AMAZING GRACE

A Country Salute to Great Gospel Hymns

FEATURING STORIES & INSIGHTS FROM

John Anderson, John Berry, Suzanne Cox,
Charlie Daniels, Billy Dean, Paul Overstreet,
Marty Rayborn, Lari White, and more

with Melissa Riddle

COUNTRYMAN ®

A Division of Thomas Nelson Publishers
Since 1798

*Hymns are
a musical profession
of our faith*

CHARLIE DANIELS

INTRODUCTION

The history of a people is found in its songs.
GEORGE JELLINEK

Trace the history of just about anything—and if you have ears to hear the stories and eyes to see the joy and sorrow, the courage and dignity, beneath the words on the page—and even the hardest skeptic can see the hand of God at work.

That is especially true of the history behind songs written for one specific purpose: to reveal the glory of God in the lives of His people. Songs that shout praises for God's grace. Songs written to God in the wake of indescribable loss. Songs filled with the hope of heaven. Songs about simple trust. Songs of gratitude and blessing. Songs that calm our fears. Songs that sing us to sleep in peace.

These gospel hymns are not bound by the constraints of a single lifetime. The faith that inspired these songs, that guided the poets and hymn writers of days gone by, lives on from generation to generation, proclaiming that God IS. And that the world truly is in His hands.

As you explore the history and timelessness of these amazing hymns, we hope you'll take the time to consider the impact they've had in your life. Revisit memories of your childhood when these songs first echoed in your ears. Or if these songs are new to you, listen to the CD as you read, and absorb the lyrics as you go. You'll discover pieces of your own experience in the passionate truths of the songs, gems you'll carry with you from this day forward. After all, "Amazing Grace" is only the beginning . . .

AMAZING GRACE

John Newton, 1779

Performed by Lari White

Grace is the free, undeserved goodness and favour of God to mankind.

MATTHEW HENRY

AFTER THE ULTIMATE STORM

John Newton was a restless young man, the kind who always seemed to get into trouble. After a miserable stint in the British Navy, he deserted, was captured, flogged, and demoted. His life was so out of control, he wound up a slave planting lime trees in Sierra Leone for almost a year. For many years after that, he made his living at sea as a slave trader, unmoved by such a despicable way of life. Until March 9, 1748. That night, a blinding storm arose off the coast of Newfoundland, and Newton could do nothing to save himself or his crew, except cry out to God for mercy. The gracious, loving God he remembered from his mother's faith not only spared Newton's life, but also led him to a new way of living.

Years later, as an anti-slavery activist and one of the most influential evangelists of his day, Newton wrote, "That tenth of March is a day much remember be me. I have never suffered it to pass unnoticed since the year 1748—the Lord came to me on high and delivered me out of deep waters."

"Amazing Grace," John Newton's very personal story of transformation, is the most famous of hundreds of hymns he penned throughout his life. It was the story of his life, and perhaps the most famous hymn of all time.

'It's a song about all of us'
LARI WHITE

Before I ever recorded "Amazing Grace," I remember that I was playing some really tiny bar in Savannah, Georgia, where it was smoky and thick, and people had been drinking. It was a hard-core country bar. The show went really well, and they asked for an encore, so I came back out and did another song. Then I sang "Amazing Grace" a cappella, and it just shut the room down. It just stopped the room. Everybody ended up singing with me, and it was like church. We had church in that bar.

One reason the song is so powerful is because the song is about grace. It meets so many people where they are, people who would never set foot in a church. It doesn't matter whether in St. Paul's Cathedral or some smoky little bar in Savannah, I have to believe that the message gets through. "Amazing Grace" had a completely different meaning at that bar in Savannah, and I think that meaning was very true to Christ's mission and why He came. He didn't come to the people who were doing it all right, all clean and polished, the shiny-happy people. He came to the people who were busted up and sick and sinful and needed help.

"Amazing Grace" is a succinct story of coming to Christ, and it's very personal. That's the common theme here—anyone who's able to be honest about themselves and their lives—even though you may be striving to do better, you're pretty conscious of what a screw-up you are. The song is just one person's experience, but in language that is so honest and truthful that everybody—millions of people for 260 years—have been moved by this song and felt like it was about them. It's a song about all of us.

THIS PASSAGE INSPIRED NEWTON'S WRITING OF 'AMAZING GRACE'

King David . . . said: "Who am I, O LORD God? And what is my house, that You have brought me this far? And yet You have also spoken of Your servant's house for a great while to come, and have regarded me according to the rank of a man of high degree, O LORD God."

1 CHRONICLES 17:16, 17

In Him we have redemption through His blood, the forgiveness
of sins, according the riches of His grace.

EPHESIANS 1:7

But may the God of all grace, who called us to His eternal glory
by Christ Jesus, after you have suffered for a while, perfect,
establish, strengthen and settle you.

1 PETER 5:10

*"God is more forgiving that we can imagine. His continuing grace can take the sorry
elements of human life and use them for His blessed purposes. There is nothing more
marvelous in all the world than the power of God's grace."*

DAVID JEREMIAH

"All men who live with any degree of serenity live by some assurance of grace."

REINHOLD NIEBUHR

*"Grace is one of the most fundamental things represented in Christianity, but I don't
think Christians always get a full understanding of what grace is. It is amazing. I
prefer 'Amazing Grace' in its simplest form. It is probably the quintessential hymn of
all time. To me, it talks about the most powerful gift that we have—grace."*

BILLY DEAN

HYMN NOTES

John Newton, an ex-slave trader turned evangelist, wrote it in 1779. It was
originally titled "Faith's Review and Expectation." Some historians speculate
that the tune of "Amazing Grace" was originally sung by slaves.

The New Dictionary of Cultural Literacy defines "Amazing Grace" as "a popular
hymn." That's quite an understatement given that "Amazing Grace" has not
only been sung by millions of congregants all over the world, but has also been
recorded more than 450 times by artists as varied as Judy Collins, Elvis Presley,
Ladysmith Black Mambazo, Tiny Tim, Al Green, Johnny Cash, Rod Stewart, and
Destiny's Child.

Amazing Grace

JUST AS I AM

Charlotte Elliott, 1835

Just as I am, without one plea
But that Thy blood was shed for me,
And that Thou bidd'st me come to Thee,
O Lamb of God, I come! I come!

By the young age of 30, Charlotte Elliott (1789-1871) had become a celebrated painter and writer in her hometown of Brighton, England, but her health had deteriorated, leaving her an invalid with crippling pain and fatigue. She became bitter and angry against God.

Then a Swiss evangelist, Dr. Caesar Malan, visited the Elliott home. Charlotte wasn't thrilled with his visit and embarrassed her family with an embittered outburst at dinner when the minister asked her if she was a Christian. Malan didn't condemn or criticize her. He simply told her that she could come to God just as she was, with all her doubts, fears, anger, and bitterness. His words gripped her heart, and three weeks later, she did just what the minister had told her was possible. She brought everything she had to God.

Twelve years later, in frustration over the fact that she was physically unable to help her brother as he prepared to build St. Mary's Hall, a school for children of clergy, Charlotte wrote what has become the most famous "invitational" hymn of all time, a hymn by which millions have come to Christ.

"I am the bread of life. He who comes to Me shall never hunger, and he who believes in Me shall never thirst. . . . All that the Father gives Me will come to Me, and the one who comes to Me I will by no means cast out."

JOHN 6:35, 37

"I'll never forget the time that I got to attend a Billy Graham crusade in Nashville. 'Just As I Am' was a song I had grown up singing as a child in church—and I had heard it sung numerous times while watching one of Dr. Graham's crusades on television—but I had never felt the impact of that song so much as when I sat near the top of the coliseum in Nashville. The combination of hearing and singing that beautiful old hymn and watching as hundreds made their way down to the coliseum floor to give their lives to Christ was overwhelming. I believe that 'Just As I Am' is truly a divinely inspired piece of music. It has such simple yet profound lyrics and melody, and ironically, the song states exactly how God accepts us at the moment of salvation . . . just as we are."

BUDDY JEWEL

HYMN NOTES

Many lives have been transformed by the simple words of this profound hymn. Dora Wordsworth, daughter of William Wordsworth, asked to have the lines read to her again and again on her deathbed. Sir Henry Norman, an official in British-controlled India, came to Christ during the hymn at a meeting led by Lord Radstock. Billy Graham has used it as the invitation in his crusades and as the title of his autobiography.

*God demonstrates His own love
toward us, in that
while we were still sinners,
Christ died for us.*
ROMANS 5:8

Just As I Am

Charlotte Elliott

William B. Bradbury

1. Just as I am, with-out one plea, But that Thy blood was shed for me, And that Thou bidst me come to Thee, O Lamb of God, I come, I come!

2. Just as I am, and wait-ing not To Thee whose blood can rid my soul of one dark blot; To Thee whose blood can cleanse each spot, O Lamb of God, I come, I come!

3. Just as I am, though tossed a-bout With many a con-flict, many a doubt, Fight-ings and fears with-in, with-out, O Lamb of God, I come, I come!

4. Just as I am, poor, wretch-ed, blind; Sight, rich-es, heal-ing of the mind. Yea, all I need, in Thee to find, O Lamb of God, I come, I come!

5. Just as I am, Thou wilt re-ceive, Wilt wel-come, par-don, cleanse, re-lieve. Be-cause Thy prom-ise I be-lieve, O Lamb of God, I come, I come!

A MIGHTY FORTRESS IS OUR GOD

Martin Luther, 1529

A mighty fortress is our God, a bulwark never failing:
Our helper He, amidst the flood of mortal ills prevailing.

The most powerful hymn to come out of the Protestant Reformation, "A Mighty Fortress Is Our God" reawakened the long-dismissed concept of congregational singing in the German Church. Written by Martin Luther (1483-1546) in 1529, this military march became a battle cry for Protestants all over Europe, inspiring and strengthening the resolve of those who faced persecution and even death for their beliefs. Inspired by the beautiful imagery of Psalm 46, Martin Luther's words rang out with the truth that God was and is "our refuge and strength, a very present help in trouble."

For still our ancient foe, Doth seek to work us woe;
His craft and powers are great, and, armed with cruel hate,
On earth is not his equal.

HYMN NOTES

Originally titled "Ein' feste Burg ist unser Gott," "A Mighty Fortress Is Our God," has more than eighty English translations, the first North American printing of which appeared in the Pennsylvania Lutheran Church Book of 1868.

God is a safe place to hide, ready to help when we
need him. We stand fearless at the cliff-edge of
doom, courageous in seastorm and earthquake.

PSALM 46:1, 2, MSG

*"Next to the Word of God, the noble art of music is the greatest treasure in the world. It
controls our thoughts, minds hearts and spirits. . . . A person who does not regard
music as a marvelous creation of God . . . does not deserve to be called a human being."*

MARTIN LUTHER

The LORD is my light and my salvation;
Whom shall I fear?
The LORD is the strength of my life;
Of whom shall I be afraid?
Though an army may encamp against me,
My heart shall not fear;
Though war should rise against me,
In this I will be confident.

PSALM 27:1, 3

Then I pray to you, O LORD.
I say, "You are my place of refuge.
You are all I really want in life."

PSALM 142:5 NLT

A Mighty Fortress Is Our God

Martin Luther   Martin Luther

1. A might-y for-tress is our God. A bul-wark nev-er fail - ing;
2. Did we in our own strength con-fide, Our striv-ing would be los - ing,
3. And though this world with dev - ils filled, Should threat-en to un-do us,
4. That word a-bove all earth - ly powers, No thanks to them, a-bid - eth;

Our help-er He a-mid the flood Of mor-tal ills pre - vail - ing.
Were not the right man on our side, The man of God's own choos - ing.
We will not fear, for God hath willed, His truth to tri - umph through us.
The Spir-it and the gifts are ours Through Him who with us sid - eth.

For still our an - cient foe Doth seek to work us woe- His craft and power are
Dost ask who that may be? Christ Je - sus, it is He- Lord Sab - a - oth His
The prince of dark-ness grim, We trem-ble not for him- His rage we can en-
Let goods and kin-dred go, This mor-tal life al - so- The bo - dy they may

great, And, armed with cru - el hate, On earth is not His e - qual.
name, From age to age the same, And He must win the bat - tle.
dure, For lo, his doom is sure: One lit - tle word shall fell him.
kill; God's truth a - bid-eth still: His king-dom is for - ev - er.

PEACE IN THE VALLEY

Thomas A. Dorsey, 1937

Performed by John Anderson

FROM THE FATHER OF GOSPEL MUSIC

With one foot in jazz, rhythm and blues and the other in the church, Thomas Dorsey bridged spiritual and blues music. Dubbed the "father of gospel music," he is said to have coined the term for the genre once known as hymns or spirituals.

The son of a traveling preacher and a church organist, Dorsey left his church and was first known as "Georgia Tom" and "Barrelhouse Tom" for his barrelhouse blues piano playing in speakeasies and after-hours parties.

Dorsey returned to his faith, writing his first spiritual songs in the early '20s, but he continued to straddle the secular and the sacred. Many churches rejected his unique style, and the financial pull of blues was strong. "I've been thrown out of some of the best churches in America," he once said.

His life took a sudden turn when in August 1932, Dorsey's wife died during childbirth, and his son passed soon after. Turning to his piano in his grief, he wrote perhaps his best-known song, "Take My Hand, Precious Lord."

Six years later, Dorsey teamed with an aspiring and dynamic singer named Mahalia Jackson, and it is with her in mind that he penned the classic "Peace in the Valley." The song is said to have been inspired by an old slave song, "We Shall Walk Through the Valley of Peace."

> I will give peace in the land, and you shall lie down,
> and none will make you afraid;
> I will rid the land of evil beasts,
> And the sword will not go through your land.
>
> LEVITICUS 26:6

'A whole lot of what the gospel is about'

JOHN ANDERSON

The overall message of "Peace in the Valley" is so plain and clear, about a sinner who believes maybe one day he'll have a spot in heaven. To me, that's a whole lot of what the gospel is about.

"Peace in the Valley" is definitely one of my favorite hymns, and I was particularly proud of this cut, too. I recorded it with my road band, back in the days when that was frowned upon; usually they used studio musicians. It was actually recorded in the late '80s for one of my Warner Brothers projects. I have always tried to throw in a gospel song on nearly every project, and this was one of those that actually made the album. In the time when I sang this song, I was just looking to express a little bit of thanks to the Lord for all the blessings that I'd received in the country music business.

HYMN NOTES

Written by Thomas A. Dorsey, known as the Father of Gospel Music, in 1937 or 1939.

Gordon Stoker of The Jordanaires tells that the producers of the Ed Sullivan Show *did not want young rocker Elvis Presley to sing a gospel song on the show. But Elvis had promised his mother, Gladys, and he performed "Peace in the Valley" on television just a few weeks before he recorded it in the studio.*

"Peace in the Valley" gained enormous popularity as a hit in numerous genres—from Mahalia Jackson's original version that was popular during World War II, to Elvis' widely popular recording, to Red Foley's take that became a country music hit.

"Peace in the Valley" was a favorite song of Dr. Martin Luther King, who asked that it be sung during the rally he led the night before his assassination.

"I will make a covenant of peace with them, and cause wild beasts to cease from the land; and they will dwell safely in the wilderness and sleep in the woods. I will make them and the places all around My hill a blessing; and I will cause showers to come down in their season; there shall be showers of blessing. Then the trees of the field shall yield their fruit, and the earth shall yield her increase. They shall be safe in their land; and they shall know that I am the LORD, when I have broken the bands of their yoke and delivered them from the hand of those who enslaved them. And they shall no longer be a prey for the nations, nor shall beasts of the land devour them; but they shall dwell safely, and no one shall make them afraid. I will raise up for them a garden of renown, and they shall no longer be consumed with hunger in the land, nor bear the shame of the Gentiles anymore. Thus they shall know that I, the LORD their God, am with them, and they, the house of Israel, are My people," says the LORD GOD. "You are My flock, the flock of My pasture; you are men, and I am your God," says the LORD GOD.

EZEKIEL 34:25-31

"I remember one time I was playing guitar at a Pentecostal church. I was about 17 years old at the time, maybe 16. I was raised Episcopalian, and had never really been at a Pentecostal church. It was a big change for me, as you can well imagine! At first I got a little bit frightened, but I learned they were just worshiping like anyone else, and I became at ease and actually started getting into my guitar playing. They were singing a lot of the old favorites that night, including 'When the Roll is Called Up Yonder' and 'What A Mighty God We Serve.'"

JOHN ANDERSON

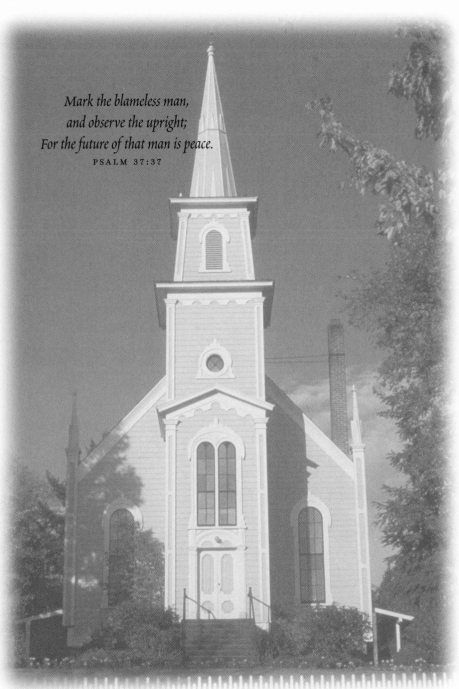

Mark the blameless man,
and observe the upright;
For the future of that man is peace.

PSALM 37:37

As for God,
His way is perfect;
The word of the LORD is proven;
He is a shield
to all who trust in Him.

PSALM 18:30

Oh, clap your hands, all you peoples!
Shout to God with the voice of triumph!
Sing praises to God, sing praises!
Sing praises to our King, sing praises!
For God is the King of all the earth;
Sing praises with understanding.

PSALM 47:1, 6, 7

NOTHING BUT THE BLOOD

Robert Lowry, 1876

What can wash away my sin? Nothing but the blood of Jesus;
What can make me whole again? Nothing but the blood of Jesus.
Oh, precious is the flow that makes me white as snow;
No other fount I know, Nothing but the blood of Jesus.

WORD PICTURES & PASSION FOR THE GOSPEL

The deepest desire of Robert Lowry (1826-1899) was to be a minister who preached the gospel, and he pursued that calling passionately, using his many gifts in pastoring Baptist churches throughout the Eastern United States in the mid 1800s. One of his most remarkable gifts, according to those who heard him preach, was his ability to paint word pictures. His vivid descriptions thrilled and inspired parishioners.

But it was his penchant for writing hymns for which he is best remembered. Although little is known about the circumstances that led Lowry to pen "Nothing But the Blood," without a doubt this simple two-chord, five-note song has garnered an important place in Church hymnody. Lowry first published this hymn in 1876, and it's likely this humble man never understand the significance of this song's impact on generations of Christians.

Lowry also composed music for many beloved classics written by Fanny Crosby, and he is perhaps best remembered for the classic hymn "Shall We Gather At the River."

If we walk in the light as He is in the light, we have fellowship with one another, and the blood of Jesus Christ His Son cleanses us from all sin.

1 JOHN 1:7

"Music, with me has been a side issue. . . . I would rather preach a gospel sermon to an appreciative audience than write a hymn. I have always looked upon myself as a preacher and felt a sort of depreciation when I began to be known more as a composer."

R O B E R T   L O W R Y

"When I moved to Nashville in the early '70s, a lot of the country shows featured a gospel portion of the show. That was part of the way we came up in country music. Once I really got involved in country music and moved to Nashville, I was glad to have what gospel background I had, because that became an important part of a lot of shows. And indeed, in our early shows, and even sometimes today, we sometimes throw in a gospel song."

J O H N   A N D E R S O N

He who believes in the Son has everlasting life; and he who does not believe the Son shall not see life, but the wrath of God abides on him.

JOHN 3:36

H Y M N   N O T E S

Robert Lowry's most popular hymn, "Shall We Gather At the River," although often sung at baptismal services, is actually a picture of heaven. He wrote it in the sweltering heat of a New York City summer in 1864.

And according to the law
almost all things are purified
with blood, and without
the shedding of blood
there is no remission.

HEBREWS
9:22

Nothing But the Blood of Jesus

Robert Lowry

Robert Lowry

What can wash a - way my sin? Noth-ing but the blood of Je - sus;
For my par - don this I see, Noth-ing but the blood of Je - sus;
Noth-ing can for sin a - tone, Noth-ing but the blood of Je - sus;
This is all my hope and peace, Noth-ing but the blood of Je - sus;

What can make me whole a - gain? Noth-ing but the blood of Je - sus.
For my cleans-ing this my plea, Noth-ing but the blood of Je - sus.
Naught of good that I have done, Noth-ing but the blood of Je - sus.
This is all my right - eous - ness, Noth-ing but the blood of Je - sus.

Refrain:

Oh! pre - cious is the flow That makes me white as snow;

No oth - er fount I know, Noth-ing but the blood of Je - sus.

THE OLD RUGGED CROSS

George Bennard, 1913

'Like seeing John 3:16 leave the printed page'

Written in 1913 by George Bennard, an ordained Methodist Episcopal minister, this hymn has become one of the most cherished of the Church. While reflecting upon his own personal trials and sufferings, Bennard (1873-1958) began to contemplate the sufferings of Jesus and the power of His cross. He was desperate for a deeper understanding of the Cross. He read and studied and meditated on the Cross until, as he later said of the experience, "It was like seeing John 3:16 leave the printed page, take form and act out the meaning of redemption. While watching this scene with my mind's eye," he said, "the theme of the song came to me. . . . The words of the finished hymn were put into my heart in answer to my own need."

"Though a preacher—a good one—[George Bennard] would sometimes sing. His voice was not trained nor out of the ordinary, but he had great feeling and expression and could really put over any hymn."

GEORGE BEVERLY SHEA

"What was relevant then is still relevant today—we all need God. A lot of people show God their love through hymns, and that's the same as it always has been. These songs are true to their meanings, they come from deep, personal places, and anything that's honest before the Lord like that, will last because those feelings, those experiences are still relevant today."

SUZANNE COX OF THE COX FAMILY

Who Himself bore our sins in His own body on the tree, that we, having died to sins, might live for right-eousness—by whose stripes you were healed.

1 PETER 2:24

"Country music and gospel music both come from rural America. All over the United States, hard-working, working-class people sang Him their songs."

JOHN ANDERSON

HYMN NOTES

George Bennard couldn't afford to have this hymn printed, so the Rev. and Mrs. L. O. Boswick, the friends for whom he first sang it, helped underwrite the initial printing costs.

"I got my start in music just going around to different
kinds of churches and playing guitar.
I loved those old songs, and always have.
'The Old Rugged Cross' is one of my favorites."

JOHN ANDERSON

The Old Rugged Cross

George Bennard

George Bennard

1. On a hill far a-way Stood an old rug-ged cross; The em-blem of
2. Oh, that old rug-ged cross, So de-spised by the world, Has a won-drous at-
3. To the old rug-ged cross I will ev-er be true, It's shame and re-

suf-fering and shame. And I love that old cross Where the dear-est and best,
trac-tion for me; For the dear Lamb of God, Left His glo-ry a-bove,
proach glad-ly bear; Then He'll call me some day To my home far a-way,

For a world of lost sin-ners was slain.
To bear it to dark Cal-va-ry. So I'll cher-ish the old rug-ged
Where His glo-ry for-ev-er I'll share.

cross, Till my tro-phies at last I lay down; I will cling to the

old rug-ged cross, And ex-change it some day for a crown.

BLESSED ASSURANCE

Fanny J. Crosby, 1873

Performed by John Berry

A LIFE OF INNER LIGHT

Blind since six weeks of age, Fanny Crosby did not let her disability stop her from being one of the most prolific hymn writers in history, and one of the best-known women of her time. "It seemed intended by the blessed providence of God that I should be blind all my life, and I think Him for the dispensation," she said. "If perfect earthly sight were offered me tomorrow, I would not accept it. I might not have sung hymns to the praise of God if I had been distracted by the beautiful and interesting things about me."

Crosby wrote her first hymn in 1864, and that same year she also wrote one of her first to become known worldwide, "Pass Me Not, O Gentle Savior." Although sources differ, probably because of the pseudonyms she often used so that her name wouldn't dominate hymnals, Fanny Crosby is known to have written between an astounding 8,000 and 9,000 hymns. As a lyricist and poet, she was paid only about $2 per song by the firm of Bigelow and Main for use of her songs in their Sunday school publications. She worked for them for several decades, penning an estimated 5,500 songs just for that company, and she often donated the money she earned to mission work.

At times, musician friends would compose music and ask Crosby to write words to complement their songs. Such was the case with Mrs. Joseph (Phoebe) Knapp, the daughter of a noted Methodist evangelist. After playing through the song on the piano, Knapp asked Crosby what the song made her feel. It is said that after praying, Crosby rose to her feet and said simply, "Why, that music says, 'Blessed assurance! Jesus is mine!'" The words "blessed assurance" continued to ring through her head during the night, and by the next morning the words to the song were complete.

'That stirs the soul'

JOHN BERRY

"Blessed Assurance" is one of my favorite hymns, and it also was my mother's favorite. She passed away in 1981.

My particular cut on the *Amazing Grace* album, "Blessed Assurance," got played every morning on the *Moby in the Morning* syndicated country radio show. In fact, every time I do an interview with him, he says, "John, sing us a verse of 'Blessed Assurance.'"

This format—as country music—brought these songs to light in a new way, and a lot of people who listen may not be in church and may not have a relationship with the Lord on a day-to-day basis. That stirs the soul. When I was a part of this record, that was my prayer—that people would hear it and that the Spirit would stir people's souls and bring about revival in them.

Why does "Blessed Assurance" stand the test of time after 100 years? If I knew that I'd be writing another one like it! There's just something about certain melodies in songs that endure. And of course the sentiment of this song is just right on.

I was asked to sing at country pioneer Hank Snow's memorial service at the Grand Ole Opry House. It was really an honor. His son called and asked me to sing a song of Hank's that I'd recorded. I asked him if he'd heard the song, and he said "no." I told him I didn't think it would be appropriate. To make a long story short, the song was "Going 90 Miles An Hour Down a Dead End Street." He said, "Oooh. I don't think so either." So I suggested "Blessed Assurance" instead, and he said it would be great.

HYMN NOTES

Written by prolific songwriter Frances Jane (Fanny) Crosby in 1873.
The first verse to the song is carved on Fanny Crosby's gravestone in Bridgeport, Connecticut.
The hymn was sung in the 1985 Academy Award® winning movie Trip to Bountiful.

The work of righteousness will be peace,
And the effect of righteousness, quietness
and assurance forever.
My people will dwell in a peaceful habitation,
In secure dwellings, and in quiet resting places.

ISAIAH 32:17, 18

*Let us draw near to God with a sincere
heart in full assurance of faith....
Let us hold unswervingly to the hope we
profess, for he who promised is faithful.*
HEBREWS 10:22-23

Blessed Assurance

Fanny J. Crosby

Phoebe P. Knapp

1. Bless-ed as - sur-ance, Je - sus is mine! Oh, what a fore-taste of
2. Per - fect sub - mis-sion, per-fect de - light! Vi - sions of rap-ture now
3. Per - fect sub - mis-sion, all is at rest. I in my Sav - ior am

glo - ry di -vine! Heir of sal - va - tion, pur - chase of God,
burst at my sight! An - gels de - scend - ing bring from a - bove
hap - py and blest; Watch - ing and wait - ing, look - ing a - bove,

Born of His Spir - it, washed in His blood! This is my sto - ry,
Ech - oes of mer - cy, whis - pers of love.
Filled with His good - ness, lost in His love.

this is my song, Prais-ing my Sav - ior all the day long. This is my

sto - ry, this is my song, Prais-ing my Sav-ior all the day long.

'TIS SO SWEET TO TRUST IN JESUS

Louisa M. R. Stead, 1882

THE HEART OF A WIDOW

Louisa M.R. Stead (1850-1917) came to America from Dover, England. She married a godly man, and they both committed their lives to serving the Lord. While having a family picnic at the beach on Long Island, New York, tragedy befell the couple. Some stories indicate that Mr. Stead attempted to rescue a drowning boy and neither survived. Other accounts say Stead rescued the boy but didn't survive. Still others suggest that Stead drowned while rescuing his and Louisa's own daughter, Lily. Either way, the death of her husband was a tragic loss.

Shortly thereafter, Louisa set out for missionary service in South Africa, a calling she'd long set aside due to frail health. While there, with Lily and her fresh grief in tow, Louisa penned the words to this great song. The year was 1882.

William J. Kirkpatrick, a gospel songwriter of the nineteenth century, wrote the melody for Louisa's hymn, which grew in popularity throughout the United States while Louisa dedicated her life to sharing the gospel overseas. Kirkpatrick's other popular hymn compositions include "Lord, I'm Coming Home," "He Hideth My Soul," "Redeemed," and "Jesus Saves."

By the time she retired from mission service in 1911, Louisa (who later married a Methodist preacher who shared her call to missions) had served more than twenty-five years on foreign soil.

"One cannot in the face of the peculiar difficulties help saying, 'Who is sufficient for these things?' but with simple confidence and trust we may and do say, 'Our sufficiency is of God.'"

LOUISA STEAD WODEHOUSE

UPON RETURNING TO MISSION SERVICE IN RHODESIA IN 1901

Trust in the LORD with all your heart, and lean not on your own understanding; In all your ways acknowledge Him, and He shall direct your paths.

PROVERBS 3:5, 6

"This has been one of my favorite songs since I was a little girl, and I was honored to even be asked to contribute to the Amazing Grace 3 record. "Tis So Sweet' so beautifully echoes the events of my own life—my personal struggles with complicated choices and uncertain times, and it offers a hope and peace that only comes from true faith in the Lord."

CYNDI THOMSON

HYMN NOTES

Louisa M.R. Stead's daughter, Lily, married a Methodist missionary named D. A. Carson and continued her mother's work in southern Rhodesia, which is now Zimbabwe.

"If you grew up in the country culture like I did in the heart of the South, there was a lot of fun and a lot of love, but we didn't have any money. You spend a lot of time praying for relief, and praying for hope, and praying sometimes to get out of a hole or a rut. You lean on faith more than probably most people who have everything. That country culture is hard times, blue collar—and you spend a lot of time on your knees. I think country and gospel go hand in hand. The music really speaks to that group of people. That's one thing that nobody and no taxes can take away from them, is that comfort from the music, and to know that there is a God they can call upon."

BILLY DEAN

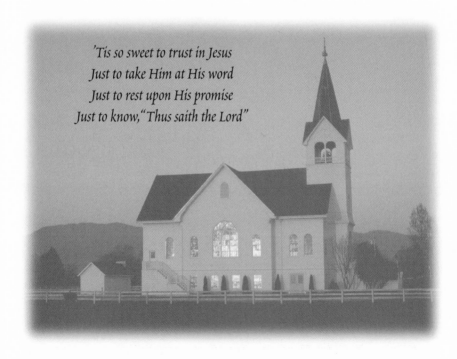

'Tis so sweet to trust in Jesus
Just to take Him at His word
Just to rest upon His promise
Just to know, "Thus saith the Lord"

'God is always faithful'

NATALIE GRANT

I remember moving to Nashville with a big dream in my heart but little money in my pocket. I had $200, no job, no car, and no place to live. I had just finished traveling with a musical touring group called Truth, and I knew that God had called me to start my own full-time ministry. I really didn't have any of the details worked out, but Divine Providence was leading the way.

From the time I was a small girl growing up in the church, I had such a love for old hymns. Even though traditional hymns were not the typical music for my generation, I am so grateful I was raised in a church that gave me an appreciation for them. Now, at this particular point in my life taking a major leap of faith by moving to Nashville, "'Tis So Sweet To Trust In Jesus" had become my theme song! There were many nights when I would find myself reciting those words as my statement of faith. God provided for me in miraculous ways those first few months. A family opened their home and gave me a place to live, and I got a part-time job. After several months, I moved out on my own. I finally got my first record deal and things were moving along like a dream, but money was really tight. It would be awhile before I started touring, and I didn't quite have enough to pay my bills. But I knew that my God never let me down. I knew that I was walking in His will, and I knew that He would provide.

One hot August afternoon. I had just added up my bills and found that I was $900 short. As I walked to my mailbox I remember praying for God's provision. As I went through the mail I noticed an envelope that looked like a personal note. I loved receiving correspondence from home! When I opened that envelope, there inside was a check for $900—the exact amount I needed, not a penny less or a penny more! This generous donation was made by someone who said that God had laid me on their heart and had prompted them to give me this amount.

God is always on time.

God is always faithful, and He never goes back on His Word.

Teach me to do Your will,
For You are my God;
Your Spirit is good.
Lead me in the land of uprightness.
PSALM 143:10

'Tis So Sweet to Trust in Jesus

Louisa M. R. Stead

William J. Kirkpatrick

1. 'Tis so sweet to trust in Je - sus, Just to take Him at His word;
2. O how sweet to trust in Je - sus, Just to trust His cleans - ing blood;
3. Yes, 'tis sweet to trust in Je - sus, Just from sin and self to cease;
4. I'm so glad I learned to trust Thee, Pre-cious Je - sus, Sav - ior friend;

Just to rest up - on His prom - ise; Just to know "Thus saith the Lord."
Just in sim - ple faith to plunge me, Neath the heal - ing, cleans - ing flood!
Just from Je - sus sim - ply tak - ing Life and rest and joy and peace.
And I know that Thou art with me, Wilt be with me to the end.

Je - sus, Je - sus how I trust Him! How I've proved Him o'er and o'er!

Je - sus, Je - sus, pre - cious Je - sus! O for grace to trust Him more!

TRUST AND OBEY

John H. Sammis, 1887

GOD'S DESIRE FOR ALL PEOPLE

Daniel B. Towner (1850-1919) was leading the music for Dwight L. Moody's evangelistic services in Massachusetts, when, as the story goes, a young man rose from his seat to give a testimony. "I am not quite sure," the young man said, "but I am going to trust, and I am going to obey." Towner wrote down the sentiments of the young man and promptly sent them off to John H. Sammis (1846-1919), a Presbyterian minister. The young man's testimony inspired the minister to write a poem based on the phrase, "trust and obey" and then sent it back to Towner to write the music.

Writing the music proved no easy task for Towner, who worked for many nights on the composition, only to throw the work in the trash can. The next morning, Towner's wife retrieved the crumpled manuscript from the trash and encouraged her husband to keep working on it. He did, and the rest is hymn history.

This simple song has translated God's desire for all people: if we place our trust in Him and obey His commandments then we can experience all the joy and happiness for which He has created us.

"I feel the melody you have written is just what is needed to carry the message."

DANIEL TOWNER'S WIFE

SAID OF THE ORIGINAL SCORE, WHICH HER HUSBAND HAD TOSSED ASIDE

Has the LORD as great delight in burnt offerings and sacrifices, as in obeying the voice of the LORD? Behold, to obey is better than sacrifice, and to heed than the fat of rams.

1 SAMUEL 15:22

"I think these hymns were written without the influence of the trends that most of the time get put into modern day songs. You know, the style of the month, like a lot of the music is today. These songs were just down-to-earth, heart-felt spiritual emotion, and what the writer felt was true."

PAUL OVERSTREET

Who among you fears the LORD?
Who obeys the voice of His Servant?
Who walks in darkness
And has no light?
Let him trust in the name of the LORD
And rely upon his God.

ISAIAH 50:10

HYMN NOTES

As the head of the Music Department at Moody Bible Institute in Chicago, Dr. Towner wrote many popular hymns including "At Calvary," "Grace Greater Than All Our Sin," and "My Anchor Holds." He died at age 70, after suffering a seizure during a revival meeting in Missouri.

*All these blessings shall come upon you
and overtake you, because you obey the
voice of the LORD your God.*

DEUTERONOMY 28:2

Trust and Obey

John H. Sammis

Daniel B. Towner

1. When we walk with the Lord In the light of His Word, What a glo-ry He
2. Not a shad-ow can rise, Not a cloud in the skies, But His smile quick-ly
3. But we nev-er can prove The de-lights of His love Un-til all on the
4. Then in fel-low-ship sweet We will sit at His feet, Or we'll walk by His

sheds on our way! While we do His good will, He a-bides with us
drives it a-way; Not a doubt nor a fear, Not a sigh nor a
al-tar we lay; For the fa-vor He shows And the joy He beside in the way; What He says we will do, Where He sends we will

still, And with all who will Trust and o-bey.
tear. Can a-bide while we Trust and o-bey.
stows Are for them who will Trust and o-bey. Trust and o-bey, For there's
go, Nev-er fear, on-ly Trust and o-bey.

no oth-er way To be hap-py in Je-sus, But to trust and o-bey.

HOW GREAT THOU ART

Stuart K. Hine, 1923

Performed by Martina McBride

Expect great things from God.
Attempt great things for God.

WILLIAM CAREY

HOW GREAT THE JOURNEY

Sometimes the message of a song is as simple as a warm summer rain, while its journey to public notice is as complex as the many hands and countries to which it is passed. Rev. Carl Gustaf Boberg was taking an afternoon walk in the countryside on the coast of Sweden when a sudden storm came up. Caught in the thunderstorm, he was amazed by the flashes of lightning and growls of thunder, and just as awed by the peace that followed the storm. Boberg penned his thoughts in a poem, "O Sotre Gud" ("Oh Great God"), which was published in 1886. For the most part, he then forgot about his creation, until several years later during his travels. It was then he heard his words sung along with a Swedish folk tune by a church congregation.

Boberg's poem was translated into German by Manfred von Glen ("Wie gross bist Du") and then into Russian in 1927. But those versions are not the song we know today.

Stuart K. Hine was born in 1899 in England. His parents, who worshiped with The Salvation Army, dedicated him to God during a tumultuous time in history. He grew up, served in the Armed Forces, and became a missionary, ministering for many years in Poland and Czechoslovakia. It was in the early 1920s when he learned the Russian text of Boberg's poem, "O Store Gud," and the original Swedish melody.

Inspired by what he heard, while on a trip through the Carpathian mountains, Hine wrote his own original interpretation, the now famous words to "How Great Thou Art."

In 1954, Dr. J. Edwin Orr—who had first heard Hine's hymn sung by Naga tribespeople from Assam—introduced "How Great Thou Art" at a conference in California. Hal Spencer and his sister, Loretta, the children of Christian music publisher Tim Spencer, were present at the conference and heard the song. And sometime later, Stuart later granted Tim Spencer the publishing rights to his hymn, which was copyrighted in 1953 by Manna Music, Inc.

HYMN NOTES

Inspired by a poem entitled "O Sotre Gud" written by Swedish pastor Rev. Carl Gustaf Boberg in 1885, the hymn now known as "How Great Thou Art" was written by Rev. Stuart K. Hine, an English missionary to the Ukraine.

The first major American recording of "How Great Thou Art" was by Bill Carle, followed by The Spencer Family. But it was George Beverly Shea's rendition of the hymn during the Billy Graham Crusades that catapulted the song into the public consciousness. In New York in 1957, "How Great Thou Art" was performed by Shea and the crusade choir more than 100 times in 119 meetings. In 1959, it became the theme of Billy Graham's "Hour of Decision" weekly radio broadcast.

"How Great Thou Art" is considered, according to many polls taken, to be the number one hymn in Britain and America. And it is certainly one of the most recorded. There have been more than one thousand documented recordings of "How Great Thou Art, which have been used on major television programs, in theatrical productions on Broadway and in London, and in major motion pictures. In 1978, ASCAP declared it as "The All-time Outstanding Gospel Song in America."

"How Great Thou Art" has been documented as the favorite Gospel song of at least three United States presidents.

"How Great Thou Art" © 1953 S. K. Hine. Assigned to Manna Music, Inc. Renewed 1981 by Manna Music, Inc. All Rights Reserved.

God, brilliant LORD, yours is a household name. Nursing infants gurgle choruses about you, toddlers shout the songs that drown out enemy talk, and silence atheist babble. I look up at your macro-skies, dark and enormous, your handsome sky-jewelry, moon and stars mounted in their settings. Then I look at my micro-self and wonder, "Why do you bother with us? Why take a second look our way?"

PSALM 8:1–9 MSG

God's glory is on tour in the skies, God-craft on exhibit across the horizon . . .

PSALM 19:1 MSG

"The Elvis song that got me was 'How Great Thou Art.' That's what hooked me. I thought if this guy, as cool as he is, can take time out to sing about God, he's got to be pretty cool!"

BILLY DEAN

"One of my very all time favorites is 'How Great Thou Art.' I do it at every one of my shows. I just don't know that there's anything else that sounds like that or comes near that grandeur. It's one of the all time greats, there's no doubt about that. It's one of those that kind of sticks with you. I love that song. It just sums things up, kind of puts it all into perspective: 'Oh Lord my God, when I in awesome wonder / consider all the worlds Thy hands have made . . .' It expresses an awe for a God that we cannot possibly come anywhere close to imagining His greatness. There's no way my little finite mind can possibly imagine what You are, and that You're everywhere, that You're everything. So 'How Great Thou Art' kind of encompasses what it's all about for me. If I could only sing one hymn the rest of my life, I think it'd probably be that one."

CHARLIE DANIELS

How Great Thou Art

Carl Boberg

Swedish Folk Melody

1. O Lord, my God, When I in awe - some won - der, Con - sid - er
2. When thru the woods and for - est glades I wan - der, And hear the
3. And when I think that God, His Son not spar - ing, Sent Him to
4. When Christ shall come With shout of ac - cla - ma - tion And take me

all the worlds Thy hands have made; I see the stars, I hear the roll - ing
birds sing sweet - ly in the trees; When I look down from loft - y moun - tain
die, I scarce can take it in; That on the cross my bur - den glad - ly
home, What joy shall fill my heart! Then I shall bow In hum - ble ad - o -

thun - der, Thy pow'r through - out The u - ni - verse dis - played.
gran - deur And hear the brook and feel the gent - le breeze.
bear - ing, He bled and died To take a - way my sin.
ra - tion, And there pro - claim, "My God, how great Thou art!"

Then sings my soul, My Sav - ior God, to Thee, How great Thou art! How great Thou art!

Then sings my soul, My Sav - ior God, to Thee, How great Thou art! How great Thou art!

BE STILL MY SOUL

Katharina A. von Schlegel, 1752

Be still, my soul. The Lord is on thy side;
Bear patiently the cross of grief or pain.
Leave to thy God to order and provide;
In every change He faithful will remain.
Be still, my soul—thy best, thy heavenly Friend
Through thorny ways leads to a joyful end.

GOD'S SUSTAINING POWER

Not much is known about the origins of this beloved hymn, but for more than 150 years it has endured as a tribute to God's sustaining power in times of trouble. No wonder it becomes more precious as our world grows more troubled.

This hymn was loved by Scottish athlete Eric Liddell, who became famous for refusing to run on the Sabbath Day in the 1924 Olympics. The award-winning movie *Chariots of Fire* depicts the events of his early life. Liddell went on to become a missionary in China, where he was imprisoned during World War II. During his imprisonment, Liddell taught his favorite hymn to other prisoners in the camp, along with his other acts of ministry.

One Sunday afternoon in February 1945, the Salvation Army band that often played outside the prison camp hospital received a note from one of the nurses: "Eric Liddell would like you to play 'Finlandia,'" which is the name of the tune t o this hymn. The band honored his request. One week later, Liddell died of a brain aneurysm and was buried outside the prison gates.

Thus says the LORD:
"Stand in the ways and see,
And ask for the old paths, where the good way is,
And walk in it;
Then you will find rest for your souls."

JEREMIAH 6:16

"We can buck up and face the music of a crisis magnificently, but it does require the supernatural grace of God to live twenty-four hours of the day as a saint, to go through drudgery as a saint, to go through poverty as a saint, unnoted and unnoticeable."

OSWALD CHAMBERS

Now may the God of peace Himself sanctify you completely; and may your whole spirit, soul, and body be preserved blameless at the coming of our Lord Jesus Christ. He who calls you is faithful, who also will do it.

1 THESSALONIANS 5:23, 24

HYMN NOTES

Words: Katharina A. von Schlegel, (1697-1768), translated from German to English by Jane Borthwick, Hymns From the Land of Luther, *1855*
Music: "Finlandia," Jean Sibelius, (1865-1957)

Be still, and know that I am God;
I will be exalted among the nations,
I will be exalted in the earth!

PSALM 46:1

Be Still, My Soul

Katharina A von Schlegel   Jean Sibelius

1. Be still, my soul; the Lord is on thy side. Bear pa - tient - ly the
2. Be still, my soul; thy God doth un - der - take To guide the fut - ure
3. Be still, my soul; the hour is hast' - ning on When we shall be for -

cross of grief or pain; Leave to thy God to or - der and pro - vide,
as He has the past. Thy hope, thy con-fi-dence let noth-ing shake;
ev - er with the Lord; When dis-ap-point-ment, grief, and fear are gone;

In ev - 'ry change He faith - ful will re - main. Be still, my soul; thy
All now mys - te - rious shall be bright at last. Be still, my soul; the
Sor - row for - got, love's pur - est joys re - stored. Be still, my soul; when

best, thy eav'n - ly Friend thru thorn - y ways leads to a joy - ful end.
waves and winds still know His voice who ruled them while He dwelt be - low.
change and tears are past, All safe and bless - ed, we shall meet at last.

IN THE GARDEN

C. Austin Miles, 1912

Performed by Billy Dean and Susan Ashton

A VISION OF THE RESURRECTION

In 1912, music publisher Dr. Adam Seibel asked C. Austin Miles to write a song, one that would be "sympathetic in tone, breathing tenderness in every line; one that would bring hope to the hopeless, rest for the weary, and downy pillows to dying beds."

Miles turned to his Bible, opening it to his favorite chapter, John 20, where Jesus and Mary meet outside the empty tomb. Reading the chapter again that day, Miles envisioned himself as part of the scene—literally having, as he described, a vision of that day.

> "My hands were resting on the Bible while I stared at the light blue wall. As the light faded, I seemed to be standing at the entrance of a garden, looking down a gently winding path, shaded by olive branches. A woman in white, with head bowed, hand clasping her throat, as if to choke back her sobs, walked slowly into the shadows. It was Mary. As she came to the tomb, upon which she placed her hand, she bent over to look in, and hurried away. John, in flowing robe, appeared, looking at the tomb; then came Peter, who entered the tomb, followed slowly by John. As they departed, Mary reappeared; leaning her head upon her arm at the tomb, she wept. Turning herself, she saw Jesus standing. So did I. I knew it was He. She knelt before Him, with arms outstretched and looking into his face cried 'Rabboni!'"

Awaking from the vision, he quickly and effortlessly wrote the words to "In the Garden," later adding the music.

'That's God talking to you'
BILLY DEAN

I love "In the Garden" because it takes you back to a time when you hope that God did walk with us and talk with us, before mankind separated itself. Who can't remember, ". . . and He walks with me and He talks with me"? "In The Garden" reminds us of the Garden of Eden, when God did walk with man and talk with man, and we turned away. We need to bring ourselves back there.

When I was a little kid, my dad, who was in World War II, would tell me stories about the inner voice that saved his life. One time while he was in Germany, this little voice inside him said, "Drop down in the snow." So he did. He didn't want to drop down in the snow—it was freezing cold—but he did. A bullet sang off a tree right where he had been standing. So all my life, Dad tried to get me to focus on that inner voice, and he'd tell me, "That's God talking to you." When I was a little kid, I got it—I paid attention to that. All through my childhood, that was kind of my companion. I spent a lot of time talking to that little inner voice, and it talking to me, and it wasn't really until later that I realized, "You know, maybe that is *God* talking to me."

Mary Magdalene came and told the disciples that she had seen the Lord, and that He had spoken these things to her.

JOHN 20:18

Now the LORD God had planted a garden in eastward in Eden, and there He put the man whom He had formed.

GENESIS 2:8

Jesus was in a garden,
not of delight as the first Adam,
in which he destroyed himself and the whole human race,
but in one of agony, in which He saved Himself
and the whole human race.

BLAISE PASCAL

"Whatever it is, that little voice has always been with me—it's the same, it's
consistent. I feel like that character in "In the Garden." I've had that happen to me
all my life. When I hear that song, it reminds me to tune that voice back in again. It's
such a sweet setting—in this beautiful garden with the dew on the roses—it's just a
peaceful, good feeling."

BILLY DEAN

In the Garden

C. Austin Miles

C. Austin Miles

1. I come to the gar-den a-lone, While the dew is still on the
2. He speaks, and the sound of His voice is so sweet, the birds hush their
3. I'd stay in the gar-den with Him, Though the night a-round me be

ros-es; And the voice I hear, fall-ing on my ear, The
sing-ing, And the mel-o-dy that He gave to me, With-
fall-ing, But He bids me go; through the voice of woe, His

Son of God dis-clos-es.
in my heart is ring-ing. And He walks with me, And He
voice to me is call-ing.

talks with me, And He tells me I am His own; And the

joy we share as we tar-ry there, None oth-er has ev-er known.

MANSION OVER THE HILLTOP

Ira F. Stanphill, 1948

Performed by Paul Overstreet

I'm satisfied with just a cottage below, / A little silver and a little gold;
But in that city where the ransomed will shine / I want a gold one that's silver-lined.

I've got a mansion just over the hilltop / In that bright land where we'll never grow old;
And someday yonder we will never more wander, / But walk the streets that are purest gold.

 'The rewards for those who endure'

PAUL OVERSTREET

When they first started talking about doing the *Amazing Grace* albums, I thought of many songs that I would like to sing, but they were already chosen by other artists. So, I went through a hymnal that I had at home and found several songs that I thought could sound like country music to me. I have always loved "Mansion Over the Hilltop," ever since singing it in church as a child. One of the album's producers called it the "I Want It All" song. It just really speaks of the earthly struggles we go through and also about the rewards for those who endure the hardships of this life.

What a great and laudable exchange to leave the things of time for those of eternity, to choose the things of heaven for the good of earth, to receive the hundredfold in place of one and to possess a blessed and eternal life.

CLARE OF ASSISI

Eye has not seen, nor ear heard,
Nor have entered into the heart of man
The things which God has prepared for those who
love Him.

1 CORINTHIANS 2:9

"When it comes to music, there's nothing like gospel. Nothing can change it. And even people who don't believe it don't take offense if it's real and honest. Bluegrass is more family–rooted. But gospel has always been a huge part of our show. We keep it as a family belief. We walk the way we talk, and it's tasteful, wholesome music for the family."

SUZANNE COX OF THE COX FAMILY

"In My Father's house are many mansions; if it were
not so, I would have told you. I go to prepare a place
for you. And if I go and prepare a place for you, I will
come again and receive you to Myself; that where I
am, there you may be also."

JOHN 14:2, 3

HYMN NOTES

Words and music written by Ira F. Stanphill. Originally recorded by Red Foley in 1953; Recorded by Elvis Presley in 1960.

His compassions fail not,
They are new every morning;
Great is Your faithfulness.
LAMENTATIONS 3:22, 23

Let all those rejoice who put their trust in You;
Let them ever shout for joy, because You defend them;
Let those also who love Your name
Be joyful in You.
For You, O LORD, will bless the righteous;
With favor You will surround him as with a shield.

PSALM 5:11, 12

JESUS PAID IT ALL

Elvina M. Hall, 1865

DISTRACTED DURING A SERMON

On an ordinary Sunday morning in 1865, Elvina M. Hall (1822-1889) was sitting in the choir section at Monument Street Methodist Church, in Baltimore, Maryland, the same place she sat every Sunday. While her pastor spoke about what Jesus had done on people's behalf, her heart was stirred with the thought that Jesus had paid it all—everything we owed, our sin-debt, our transgressions, our iniquities, our punishment, everything. Jesus came and paid the price for our redemption.

As the preacher prayed, Elvina quickly wrote out her thoughts on the inside cover of one of the choir hymnbooks. When she shared the poem with the coal miner who served as the church organist, John T. Grape (1835-1915), he agreed to compose a melody for it. And thus, although it would not be published for almost fourteen more years, a timeless hymn was born—a treasured song of redemption that was certainly worth the wait.

You were not redeemed with corruptible things, like silver or gold, from your aimless conduct received by tradition from your fathers, but with the precious blood of Christ, as of a lamb without blemish and without spot.

1 PETER 1:18-19

"If you want to be perfect, go, sell what you have and give to the poor, and you will have treasure in heaven; and come, follow Me."

MATTHEW 19:21

I thank my God always concerning you for the grace of God which was given to you by Christ Jesus, that you were enriched in everything by Him in all utterance and all knowledge, even as the testimony of Christ was confirmed in you, so that you come short in no gift, eagerly waiting for the revelation of our Lord Jesus Christ, who will also confirm you to the end, that you may be blameless in the day of our Lord Jesus Christ God is faithful, by whom you were called into the fellowship of His Son, Jesus Christ our Lord.

1 CORINTHIANS 1:4-9

HYMN NOTES

Monument Street Methodist Church was being renovated at the time Elvina Hall wrote her hymn. The church organ had been moved to the home of organist John T. Grape. Otherwise, Grape, who was a coal miner for five days of the week, might not have had time to compose the tune.

But God demonstrates His own love toward us,
in that while we were still sinners, Christ died for us.

ROMANS 5:8

Jesus Paid It All

Elvina M. Hall

John T. Grape

1. I hear the Sav - ior say, "Thy strength in - deed is small;
2. Lord, now in - deed I find, Thy power and Thine a - lone;
3. For noth-ing good have I, Where - by Thy grace to claim;
4. And when be - fore the throne, I stand in Him com - plete;

Child of weak-ness watch and pray, Find in Me thine all in all."
Can change the lep - er's spots And melt the heart of stone.
I'll wash my gar-ments white, In the blood of Cal-vary's Lamb.
"Je - sus died my soul to save," My lips shall still re - peat.

Je - sus paid it all, all to Him I owe;

Sin had left a crim-son stain, He washed it white as snow.

TAKE MY LIFE AND LET IT BE

Frances Havergal, 1874

'I WAS TOO HAPPY TO SLEEP'

Frances Havergal (1836-1879) had a glorious voice and a way with words, but at age 36 she felt something was missing in her Christian life. Then, one day in 1873, she read a little book titled All For Jesus. The words pricked her heart, and she decided to consecrate every area of her life in honor of God.

Not long afterward, she would pen the words for which she would be remembered most: "Take My Life and Let It Be."

Of this beautiful hymn's origin, Frances said: "I went for a little visit of five days. There were ten persons in the house, some unconverted and long prayed for, some converted, but not rejoicing Christians. He gave me the prayer 'Lord, give me all in this house!' And He just did! Before I left the house every one had gotten a blessing . . . I was too happy to sleep and passed most of the night in praise and renewal of my own consecration; and these little couplets formed themselves, and chimed in my heart one after another till they finished with 'Ever, only, all for Thee!'"

"This hymn sums up what we all want to say to God: 'Take everything about me . . . take all I am and all I own. It's Yours, Lord.'"

CHRIS TOMLIN

I beseech you therefore, brethren, by the mercies of God, that you present your bodies a living sacrifice, holy, acceptable to God, which is your reasonable service. And do not be conformed to this world, but be transformed by the renewing of your mind, that you may prove what is that good and acceptable and perfect will of God.

ROMANS 12:1, 2

HYMN NOTES

Taking seriously the words she'd penned, "Take my silver and my gold / Not a mite would I withhold," Frances donated all her jewelry to the Church Missionary Society.

Give and it will be given to you:
good measure, pressed down,
shaken together,
and running over ...
LUKE 6:38

Take My Life and Let It Be

Frances R. Havergal

Henri A. Cesar Malan

1. Take my life and let it be Con - se - crat - ed, Lord to Thee. Take my hands and let them move, At the im - pulse of Thy love, At the im - pulse of Thy love.
2. Take my feet, and let them be Swift and beau - ti - ful for Thee. Take my voice, and let me sing Al - ways, on - ly, for my King. Al - ways, on - ly, for my King.
3. Take my lips, and let them be Filled with mes - sa - ges for Thee. Take my sil - ver and my gold; Not a mite would I with - hold, Not a mite would I with - hold.
4. Take my love, my God, I pour At Thy feet its trea - sure store. Take my - self and I will be Ev - er, on - ly, all for Thee, Ev - er, on - ly, all for Thee.

BEULAH LAND

Squire Parsons, Jr., 1979

Performed by Shenandoah

A MUSICAL HERITAGE

Squire Parsons, Jr., a native of Newton, West Virginia, was raised in a Christian home and was immersed in gospel music while still in the cradle. His father, Squire Parsons, Sr., was a choir director who taught shaped-note gospel music, and he raised his very musical family with strong gospel roots.

Always enthralled with harmonies and the caravan style of singing that was popular in that era, Squire Parsons, Jr. graduated in 1970 from West Virginia Institute of Technology where he earned a Bachelor of Science degree in music education. After graduation, Squire Jr. taught high school band for four years. It was during this time, on an ordinary morning while driving to school, that Parsons penned the first verse and chorus of his now famous hymn, "Sweet Beulah Land."

"I had not planned to write a song that morning," Parsons recalls. "I was simply singing as I was driving, having church in the car, like many of us do. I was singing an old song called 'Is Not This the Land of Beulah?' an old song that had always impressed me with its theology and its beautiful melody. That, along with the song 'Beulah Land' that was written during the Civil War era, were part of our worship at Newton Baptist Church.

"That morning in the car, he continued, "the melody and the words for a new song just started coming together. So I went to the old band room at the school, an old one-room schoolhouse that had been converted into a band room. It wasn't the most elaborate facility, but it was a wonderful experience that morning as I sat and finalized the first verse and chorus of that song."

Six years later, after his first professional stint with the popular southern gospel quartet, The Kingsmen, Parsons rediscovered the beginnings of the song as he searched for new material for his first solo album, also titled "Sweet Beulah Land." He then added the rest of the verses and sang it in public for the first time at Trinity Baptist Church in Asheville, North Carolina. It was clear, from that first live performance, that this song was different from all the others he'd written.

"I'll never forget that night. We had a little widow lady, Ma Stewart, at our church, and she was always very expressive. But that night, when I sang that song, she had herself an old-fashioned shouting experience. Everyone present had a wonderful time thinking about the glories of heaven. . . . I've been singing it ever since, and I'm just amazed that thirty years down the road, it's still what people wait to hear in my concerts. It's more precious as I grow older, more like a friend. It's just part of me. And it has certainly been an honor to sing it."

Squire Parsons, Jr. has enjoyed a successful ministry as a gospel soloist, recording more than twenty-five Southern-gospel albums to date. He still travels and performs at over 200 dates a year. He and his wife, Linda, currently reside in Leicester, North Carolina.

I'm kind of homesick for a country / To which I've never been before
No sad goodbyes will there be spoken / For time won't matter anymore.

Beulah land, I'm longing for you / And some day on thee I'll stand
There my home shall be eternal / Beulah land, sweet Beulah land

---

HYMN NOTES

Words and music written by Squire Parsons, Jr. in 1979.
"Beulah" is the beautiful land beyond the river of death in the allegorical epic Pilgrim's Progress, *written by John Bunyan in 1678.*
"Beulah" literally means "married" in the original Hebrew. The prophet Isaiah uses this word to refer to a perfected Israel in complete, joyous unity—or marriage—with God.

'It speaks of the promise we've been given'
MARTY RAYBORN, SHENANDOAH

"Beulah Land" was a song I'd been singing for some time at different churches, and I'd really seen the impact it had on people. They'd come up to me afterward and say, "Man, that song is beautiful. I just really love the way you sing that one." It became one of the most requested songs I ever sang. So when we were approached about doing a song for the *Amazing Grace* album, it was the obvious choice for us. It just speaks to people.

It speaks of the promise we've been given in God's Word—that we have hope and that one day we will literally dwell in the land of Beulah. The word "Beulah" is mentioned only one time in scripture, but that day, that place is mentioned often in the Bible. That place where He will literally be the Light of the World. He is already the Light, but on that day, in that place, he will be the only Light.

Is there an evangelistic message in this song? No. It just talks about what will become of those who love the Lord, those who believe. I've got a few more days to labor, and when that's done I'm headed to the House.

The hope of heaven seems to be more accepted among the elderly, for obvious reasons. People, saints of God, who have lived their lives already, they are ready to go. There've been times when I get into that second verse, when I sing "then I'll take my heavenly flight," I've seen old people stand up and shout "Hallelujah!" right in the middle of the song, because that's what they're waiting to do. Just thinking about it now gives me goose bumps.

"In that sweet by and by we shall meet on that beautiful shore"
PREACHER AND HYMN-WRITER IRA SANKEY (1840-1908)

You shall no longer be termed 'Forsaken,'
Nor shall your land any more be termed 'Desolate';
But you shall be called 'Hephzibah,'
and your land *'Beulah';*
For the LORD delights in you,
And your land shall be married.
For as a young man marries a virgin,
So shall your sons marry you;
And as the bridegroom rejoices over the bride,
So shall your God rejoice over you.

ISAIAH 62:4, 5

"Let us be glad and rejoice and give Him glory, for the
marriage of the Lamb has come, and His wife has
made herself ready."

REVELATION 19:7

"Short arm man needs to reach to Heaven,
so ready is Heaven to stoop to Him."
FRANCIS THOMPSON, ENGLISH POET (1859-1907)

Praise the LORD!
For it is good to sing praises to our God;
For it is pleasant, and praise is beautiful.
PSALM 147:1

"When those hymns meant something to people,
the writers didn't get paid to write that stuff.
When John Newton found Jesus, when he wrote 'Amazing
Grace,' he understood the grace of God.
When 'How Great Thou Art' was written, that writer
experienced first-hand the majesty of God. He didn't write
that to get paid. He wrote it because it revealed his
experience with the Lord....
There's nothing on earth like 'Blessed Assurance' and
'Heaven Came Down and Glory Filled My Soul,' 'Nothing
But the Blood of Jesus', and 'It Is Well With My Soul.'
When you immerse yourself in those old hymns,
you get a foretaste of what we're going to hear in heaven."

MARTY RAYBORN, SHENANDOAH

NO ONE EVER CARED FOR ME LIKE JESUS

Charles Frederick Weigle, 1932

I would love to tell you what I think of Jesus
Since I found in Him a friend so strong and true;
I would tell you how He changed my life completely,
He did something that no other friend could do.

No one ever cared for me like Jesus,
There's no other friend so kind as He;
No one else could take the sin and darkness from me,
Oh how much He cared for me.

'A TESTIMONY TO GOD'S HEALING LOVE'

This beautiful song was written by evangelist and songwriter Charles Weigle (1871-1966) during perhaps the darkest period of his life. An inspiring preacher and gifted songwriter, Charles had written more than 1,000 songs. But after returning home from a ministry trips, he found a note that his wife of many years had left him. She no longer wanted to be married to a minister, the note read.

Devastated, Charles sank into a deep depression and in the years that followed even contemplating taking his own life. He became convinced that no one cared for him, that no one could love him. Gradually his faith strengthened, and once again Charles began to sing and preach. This powerful song stands as a lasting testimony to the healing power of God's steadfast love.

"I will never leave you nor forsake you."
HEBREWS 13:5

I have been crucified with Christ; it is no longer I who live, but Christ lives in me; and the life which I now live in the flesh I live by faith in the Son of God, who loved me and gave Himself for me.
GALATIANS 2:20

HYMN NOTES

Charles Weigle spent the last fifteen years of his life teaching at Tennessee Temple schools in Chattanooga, Tennessee.

ROCK OF AGES

Augustus M. Toplady, 1776

Rock of ages, cleft for me,
Let me hide myself in Thee;

FROM REBUTTAL TO RENOWN

Many beloved and timeless hymns are born out of personal experience, the triumphs and tragedies in the lives of those who wrote them. But "Rock of Ages" is not one of those. Rather, "Rock of Ages" was written as a satirical jab in an ongoing theological debate between young Anglican minister Augustus M. Toplady of London and John and Charles Wesley, prominent Methodist evangelists.

Part of the hymn's inspiration no doubt came from the story of Moses and how God hid him in the cleft of the rock, allowing Moses to witness God's passing by. But by in large, the hymn was Toplady's way of rebuttal of the Wesleyan teachings about remorse and repentance, as well as the Armenian doctrine of sanctification. Noted hymnologist Dr. Louis J. Benson believes Toplady (1740-1778) even plagiarized portions of a hymn Charles Wesley had written thirty years prior—obviously Augustus had an ax to grind. Toplady went on to become a passionate evangelical preacher all throughout England until he died of tuberculosis at the age of 38.

The origin of this classic hymn has not kept it from becoming a favorite. From the most primitive of rural churches to the splendor of Westminster Abby, "Rock of Ages"—the tune of which was composed by American Thomas Hastings (1784-1832) in 1830—will echo through the generations as a powerful tribute to the saving grace of God.

Not by works of righteousness which we have done, but according to His mercy He saved us, through the washing of regeneration and renewing of the Holy Spirit.

TITUS 3:5

"My heart beats every day stronger and stronger for glory. Sickness is no affliction, pain no cause, death itself no dissolution. . . . My prayers are now all converted into praise."

AUGUSTUS M. TOPLADY

JUST PRIOR TO HIS DEATH

Be anxious for nothing, but in everything by prayer and supplication, with thanksgiving, let your requests be made known to God; and the peace of God, which surpasses all understanding, will guard your hearts and minds through Christ Jesus.

PHILIPPIANS 4:6, 7

HYMN   NOTES

Toplady's hymn originally appeared in The Gospel Magazine *in 1776 under the title "A Living and Dying Prayer for the Holiest Believer in the World."*

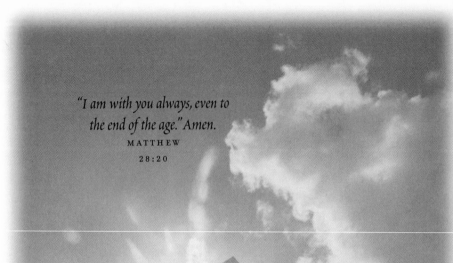

"I am with you always, even to the end of the age." Amen.

MATTHEW

28:20

Rock of Ages

Augustus M. Toplady

Thomas Hastings

1. Rock of A - ges, cleft for me, Let me
2. Could my tears for - ev - er flow? Could my
3. While I draw this fleet - ing breath, When my

hide my - self in Thee. Let the wa - ter and the
zeal no lan - guor know? These for sin could not a -
eyes shall close in death, When I rise to worlds un -

blood, From Thy wound - ed side which flowed, Be of
tone; Thou must save, and Thou a - lone. In my
known, And be - hold Thee on Thy throne, Rock of

sin the dou - ble cure, Save from wrath and make me pure.
hand no price I bring; Sim - ply to thy cross I cling.
A - ges cleft for me, Let me hide my - self in Thee.

I'D RATHER HAVE JESUS

Rhea F. Miller, 1922

Performed by Allison Krause & The Cox Family,
featuring Suzanne Cox

Jesus alone IS; the rest IS NOT.

THERESE OF LISIEUX

PERSPECTIVE AT A CROSSROADS

Born in Winchester, Ontario, the son of a church organist and a Methodist minister, George Beverly Shea grew up hearing the gospel in song. But when he was 21, his passion for singing became a viable vocational option—a means by which he could make a living. After placing second in a national competition aired on NBC, the sky was the limit. George was offered a singing job in New York City, a position that came with a great salary and wide respect. But his heart was torn between pursuing fame and fortune and following a higher call.

As the story goes, just a short time later, while sitting at the family piano to prepare a special hymn for an upcoming Sunday service, 23-year-old George discovered a clipping of a poem, obviously left for him by a wise, concerned mother. The poem had been written by Mrs. Rhea F. Miller. Immediately, the words of the poem gripped George's heart, and the melody for the poem quickly came to him. The next day, George Beverly Shea sang "I'd Rather Have Jesus" in church for the first time.

In the years that followed 1946, Shea would sing this hymn as part of the Billy Graham evangelistic crusades, of which he became an integral part. This hymn became his signature song.

A Song of Commitment & Faith
SUZANNE COX

Sometimes in life you just know it's a God-thing, and that's the way our family felt about working with Alison Krauss, recording this song for the *Amazing Grace* album.

When I first met Alison, I was 21, just a little older than she was, and I just felt a real connection with her. My family was just about to get out of the music business for awhile to regroup, and when Alison came along, she sort of re-energized us. The Cox Family's hymns album, *I Know Who Holds Tomorrow*, was a collaboration with Allison, a labor of love, one of our best efforts, and a Grammy winner. So when we had the opportunity to contribute to the *Amazing Grace* project, it was such a privilege to sing this special song with her.

Our family has often sung "I'd Rather Have Jesus" in our shows, but I first came to know it when my daddy taught it to me many years ago. I was asked to sing it for a funeral. Even back then, I just loved what it says, that somebody would be so deeply committed with God that they'd give up everything to follow Him. We live in such a materialistic world, when someone can sing such a thing as "I'd rather have Jesus than silver or gold," she'd better mean it.

When I was in my 20s doing this song, even then I felt this special connection to the words of this song. I just envisioned the words of the song, and I guess you could say I was convicted about what it said. Now that I'm older, I appreciate the lyrics even more and the impact the words have had in my life.

> "For what profit is it to a man if he gains the whole world and loses his own soul?"
> ### MATTHEW 16:26

HYMN NOTES
Music by George Beverly Shea (1909-), based on a 1922 poem written by Rhea F. Miller.
Loretta Lynn recorded "I'd Rather Have Jesus" on her Hymns album, back in 1965.

God will wipe away every tear from their eyes; there shall be no more death, nor sorrow, nor crying. There shall be no more pain, for the former things have passed away.

Then He who sat on the throne said, "Behold, I make all things new." And He said to me, "Write, for these words are true and faithful."

And He said to me, "It is done! I am the Alpha and the Omega, the Beginning and the End. I will give of the fountain of the water of life freely to him who thirsts."

REVELATION 21:4–6

When they had lifted up their eyes,
they saw no one but Jesus only.
MATTHEW 17:8

I'd Rather Have Jesus

Rhea F. Miller

George Beverly Shea

1. I'd rath-er have Je-sus than sil-ver or gold; I'd rath-er be
2. I'd rath-er have Je-sus than men's ap - plause; I'd rath-er be
3. He's fair-er than lil-ies of rar-est bloom; He's sweet-er than

His than have rich-es un-told; I'd rath-er have Je-sus than
faith-ful to His dear cause; I'd rath-er have Je-sus than
hon-ey from out the comb; He's all that my hun-ger-ing

hous-es or lands. I'd rath-er be led by His nail-pierced hand.
world-wide fame. I'd rath-er be true to His ho-ly name.
spi - rit needs. I'd rath-er have Je-sus and let Him lead.

Than to be the king of a vast do-main Or be held in sin's dread sway.

I'd rath-er have Je-sus than an-y-thing This world af-fords to-day.

I NEED THEE EVERY HOUR

Annie S. Hawks, 1872

FROM A HOUSEWIFE'S HEART

"I remember well the circumstances under which I wrote the hymn," Brooklyn, New York housewife and mother of three Annie Sherwood Hawks (1835-1918) shared of how this hymn came to life.

"It was a bright June day, and I became so filled with the sense of the nearness of my Master that I began to wonder how anyone could live without Him, in either joy or pain. Suddenly, the words 'I need Thee every hour' flashed into my mind, and very quickly the thought had full possession of me. Seating myself by the open windows, I caught up my pencil and committed the words to paper—almost as they are today."

A few weeks later, Hawks' minister, Dr. Robert Lowry (1826-1899), composed the melody for the hymn and added the refrain. The hymn was published in the Baptist hymnbook in 1873.

Sixteen years later, after the death of her husband, Annie Hawks wrote: "At first I did not understand why the hymn so greatly touched the throbbing heart of humanity. Years later, however, under the shadow of a great loss, I came to understand something of the comforting power of the words I had been permitted to give out to others in my hours of sweet serenity and peace."

Annie Hawks wrote more than 400 hymns in her lifetime. "I Need Thee Every Hour" is the best known.

Not that we are sufficient of ourselves to think of anything as being from ourselves, but our sufficiency is from God.

2 CORINTHIANS 3:5

"O Lord God who art all in all to me, Life of my life and Spirit of my spirit, have mercy on me and fill me with Thy Holy Spirit and with love that there may be no room for anything else in my heart. In Thyself alone is satisfaction and abundance for my heart; Thou Thyself, O Creator, hast created this heart for Thyself, and not for any other created thing. Therefore this heart cannot find rest in aught but Thee: only in Thee, O Father, who hast made this longing for peace. So now take out of this heart whatever is opposed to Thee and abide and rule in it Thyself, Amen."

SADHU SUNDAR SINGH

The LORD will guide you continually,
And satisfy your soul in drought.
And strengthen your bones;
You shall be like a watered garden,
and like a spring of water, whose waers do not fail.

ISAIAH 58:11

Wait on the LORD;
Be of good courage,
And He shall strengthen your heart;
wait, I say, on the LORD!

PSALM 27:14

Bow down Your ear,
O Lord, hear me;
For I am poor and needy.

PSALM 86:1

I Need Thee Every Hour

Annie S. Hawks; Robert Lowry, Refrain

Robert Lowry

1. I need Thee ev - 'ry hour, Most gra - cious Lord;
2. I need Thee ev - 'ry hour, Stay Thou near by;
3. I need Thee ev - 'ry hour In joy or pain;
4. I need Thee ev - 'ry hour, Most Ho - ly One.

No ten - der voice like Thine Can peace af - ford.
Temp - ta - tions lose their power When Thou art nigh.
Come quick - ly and a - bide Or life is vain.
Oh, make me Thine in - deed, Thou bless - ed Son!

I need Thee, O I need Thee; Ev - 'ry hour I need Thee;

O bless me now, my Sav - ior, I come to Thee!

WHAT A FRIEND WE HAVE IN JESUS

Joseph Scriven, 1855

'THE LORD AND I DID IT BETWEEN US'

Devastated by the drowning death of his betrothed on the night before their wedding, Joseph Scriven (1819-1886) migrated from Ireland to Canada, awash in grief. Ten years later, Joseph included his little poem, "What A Friend We Have In Jesus" as part of a letter sent to encourage his ailing mother in Ireland. His mother liked the poem so much, she gave it to a friend who published it, although somewhere along the way, Joseph's name was left off. Charles C. Converse (1832-1918) would eventually give the poem its melody. No one knew who wrote the words for many years, but the hymn grew in popularity.

Meanwhile, back in Canada, Joseph had met and become engaged to another young woman. She, too, died tragically before their wedding day. To deal with his profound grief, Joseph immersed himself in ministry to the poor, working with the Plymouth Bretheren. He eventually settled in Port Hope, Canada, devoting his life to helping the poor and needy. He was often thought of as eccentric because he gave away his money and clothing to help those in need.

It wasn't until much later in his life that a friend, who had come to visit Joseph who was sick, noticed the original manuscript of the poem on a piece of paper beside Joseph's bed and asked him about it. Joseph replied, "The Lord and I did it between us."

> May our Lord Jesus Christ Himself, and our God and Father, who has loved us and given us everlasting consolation and good hope by grace, comfort your hearts and establish you in every good word and work.
>
> 2 THESSALONIANS 2:16, 17

"You are My friends if you do whatever I command you.

No longer do I call you servants, for a servant does not know what his master is doing; but I have called you friends, for all things that I hearrd from My Father I have made known to you.

You did not choose Me, but I chose you and appointed you that you should go and bear fruit, and that your fruit should remain, that whate er you ask the Father in My name He may give you.

JOHN 15:14-16

"God's hearing of our prayers does not depend upon what we are in ourselves, but what we are in Christ Jesus; both our person and our prayers are acceptable in the Beloved."

ANONYMOUS

If we endure,
We shall also reign with Him.
If we deny Him, He also will deny us.
If we are faithless,
He remains faithful;
He cannot deny Himself.

2 TIMOTHY 2:12, 13

HYMN NOTES

Joseph Scriven died at age 66 and was buried facing the grave of his beloved fiancée Eliza Catherine Roche.

A man who has friends must himself be friendly, but there is a friend who sticks closer than a brother.

PROVERBS 18:24

What a Friend We Have in Jesus

Joseph M. Scriven

Charles C. Converse

1. What a Friend we have in Je-sus, All our sins and griefs to bear!
2. Have we tri-als and temp-ta-tions? Is there trou-ble an-y-where?
3. Are we weak and heav-y-lad-en, Cum-bered with a load of care?

What a priv-i-lege to car-ry, Ev-ery-thing to God in prayer!
We should nev-er be dis-cour-aged; Take it to the Lord in prayer.
Pre-cious Sav-ior, still our ref-uge! Take it to the Lord in prayer.

Oh, what peace we of-ten for-feit, Oh, what need-less pain we bear.
Can we find a friend so faith-ful, Who will all our sor-rows share?
Do Thy friends de-spise, for-sake Thee? Take it to the Lord in prayer.

All be-cause we do not car-ry Ev-ery-thing to God in prayer!
Je-sus knows our ev-ery weak-ness; Take it to the Lord in prayer.
In His arms He'll take and shield Thee; Thou wilt find a so-lace there.

KNEEL AT THE CROSS

Charles E. Moody, 1924

Performed by the Charlie Daniels Band

 'A song that had a real big place in my heart'

CHARLIE DANIELS

I grew up in a Methodist church, a God-fearing, Bible-preaching church. I was raised in small towns and rural areas and most of the people in those areas go to church—or at least back in my day they did—and I never lived in a big city until I was grown.

My family, I mean we sang. I remember people getting together at my grandmother's house around an old upright piano and singing on Sunday afternoons. That's what people used to do, visit each other. They'd get together and sing old hymns. It's just been part of my heritage for as long as I can remember. A very strong part of my heritage.

I was maybe four or five years old when I started singing in church, and my song was "Kneel at the Cross." That was my song, and it was a pretty big song for a little kid. But I learned it; it was my tune. That's what I did; that's what I sang. Of course, I didn't understand it at all. I just did it because I could.

But when it came time to choose a song for the Amazing Grace: A Country Salute to Gospel CD, it seemed like the natural choice. It was a song that had a real big place in my heart.

Satan trembles when he sees the weakest saint upon his knees.

WILLIAM COWPER

When you were spiritually dead because of your sins and because you were not free from the power of you sinful self, God made you alive with Christ, and he forgave all your sin. He canceled the debt, which listed all the rules we failed to follow. He took away that record with its rules and nailed it to the cross.

COLOSSIANS 2:13, 14 NCV

"I'd been doing gospel music in my shows for a long time before I ever recorded any of it, because we were always on major record labels. They just don't do gospel albums anymore, so I hadn't really had a chance to record gospel music. When we were approached by Sparrow, of course we went ahead and did the Amazing Grace album, but that was not my advent into gospel music; it was just my advent into the recording part of it. I had been performing it for years. I've had people ask me, 'What do you think your fans are going to think about you doing gospel?' I would reply, 'It's part of what we do, and if I can't take Jesus with me, I don't want to go.' If He can't go with me, I don't want to go anyplace that He can't be. So, if I can't sing gospel music some-where, I just won't go, it's that simple."

CHARLIE DANIELS

"The Blood of Jesus deals with what we have done, whereas the Cross deals with what we are."

WATCHMAN NEE

HYMN NOTES

Words and music written by Charles E. Moody for the Tennessee Music & Printing Company.

"Worry does not empty tomorrow of its sorrow;
it empties today of its strength."

CORRIE TEN BOOM

I believe my King suggests a thought, and whispers me a musical line or two, and then I look up and thank Him delightedly and go on with it. That is how my hymns come.

FRANCES RIDLEY HAVERGAL

Joy to all creatures,
honor, feasting, delight.
Dark death is destroyed
and life is restored everywhere.
The gates of Heaven are open.

HIPPOLYTUS

WERE YOU THERE?

African-American Spiritual

Were you there when they crucified my Lord?
Oh, sometimes it causes me to tremble, tremble, tremble.
Were you there when they crucified my Lord?

STRENGTH FOR THE SLAVES

The origins of "Were You There" are rooted in a tragic period in American history as African slaves suffered cruelty and oppression under American slave owners who often claimed to believe in God. Slave owners even used the New Testament to justify their unjust treatment of slaves, an appalling misuse of Scripture. Still, somehow, the power of the Gospel message reached down deep into the heart of the slave. Somehow this Jesus who suffered and was mistreated, as they had suffered and been mistreated, could understood their pain. He, the Son of God, had hung on a tree! And yet, this Jesus said, "Father forgive them for they do not know what they do" (Luke 23:34).

In the Cross the slaves felt the power of divine will, a dissolution of the barriers that separated man from man and man from God. They drew strength from Jesus' example of forgiveness, love, and mercy. He was all they had. He was their hope and song. These songs called "spirituals" were just that—songs that came up out of the human spirit as it cried out to God for freedom and, at once, shouted praise for God's provision. Perhaps these children of God understood His sufferings, His passion, better than most.

He is despised and rejected by men,
A Man of sorrows and acquainted with grief.
And we hid, as it were, *our* faces from Him;
He was despised, and we did not esteem Him.
Surely He has borne our griefs
And carried our sorrows;
Yet we esteemed Him stricken,
Smitten by God, and afflicted.
But He was wounded for our transgressions,
He was bruised for our iniquities;
The chastisement for our peace was upon Him,
And by His stripes we are healed.

ISAIAH 53:3—5

I determined not to know anything among you except
Jesus Christ and Him crucified. I was with you in
weakness, in fear, and in much trembling. And my
speech and my preaching were not with persuasive
words of human wisdom, but in demonstration of the
Spirit and of power, that your faith should not be in
the wisdom of men but in the power of God.

1 CORINTHIANS 2:2-5

HYMN NOTES

Some African–American religious singing before 1865 was referred as a "moan" or a "groan." But moaning or groaning, in this sense, does not imply pain. Instead, it implies a blissful rendition of a song, often mixed with humming and spontaneous melodic variation.

The LORD also will be a
refuge for the oppressed.
A refuge in times of trouble.
PSALM 9:9

Were you there

when they crucified my Lord?
Were you there when they crucified my Lord?

*O . . . sometimes it causes me
to tremble, tremble, tremble.*

Were you there when they crucified my Lord?

Were you there

. . . when they nailed Him to the tree?

. . . when the sun refused to shine?

. . . when they laid Him in the tomb?

. . . when He rose up from the grave?

WHEN I SURVEY
THE WONDROUS CROSS

Isaac Watts, 1707

When I survey the wondrous cross
On which the Prince of glory died,
My richest gain I count but loss,
And pour contempt on all my pride.

A DESIRE FOR BETTER PRAISE

Isaac Watts (1674-1748) wrote this hymn in 1707 for a Holy Communion service he was soon to conduct. The original title he had given it was, "Crucifixion to the World by the Cross of Christ." A wealthy non-conformist, Watts was vocal in his feelings about church music. He once said, "The singing of God's praise is the part of worship most closely related to heaven, but its performance among us is the worst on earth." After church one Sunday, Watts again was lamenting church music when his frustrated father replied, "Why don't you give us something better!" The impertinent son took his father's words as a challenge and did just that, touching millions with the glorious message of Christ's sacrifice for our sins.

During his lifetime Watts penned approximately 600 hymns, but most of his best efforts were turned out in the two years after his graduation from Dissenter's Academy in London and his taking a job as a teacher when he was 22. During these two years, hymns poured from this genius of hymnody. Of these, forty-three are in common use today, including "Alas And Did My Savior Bleed," "Am I A Soldier of the Cross" and "Joy to the World."

Do not love the world or the things in the world. If anyone loves the world, the love of the Father is not in him. For all that is in the world—the lust of the flesh, the lust of the eyes, and the pride of life—is not of the Father but is of the world. And the world is passing away, and the lust of it; but he who does the will of God abides forever.

1 JOHN 2:15—17

Joy to the world
the Lord is come. Let earth receive her King.
Let ev-ry heart prepare Him room.
And heav'n and nature sing.
And heav'n and nature sing.

ISAAC WATTS

HYMN NOTES

Isaac Watts' poems and songs for children were extremely popular throughout Europe, and his verse became an object of parody in Lewis Carroll's Alice in Wonderland.

But God forbid that I should boast
except in the cross of our Lord Jesus Christ,
by whom the world has been crucified to me,
and I to the world.
GALATIANS 6:14

When I Survey the Wondrous Cross

Isaac Watts

Arr. Lowell Mason

1. When I sur - vey the won - drous cross
2. For - bid it, Lord, that I should boast,
3. See, from His head, His hands, His feet,
4. His dy - ing crim - son, like a robe,
5. Were the whole realm of na - ture mine,

On which the Prince of glo - ry died,
Save in the death of Christ, my Lord;
Sor - row and love flow min - gled down;
Spreads o'er His bod - y on the tree;
That were a pres - ent far too small;

My rich - est gain I count but loss
All the vain things that charm me most
Did e'er such love and sor - row meet,
Then am I dead to all the globe,
Love so a - maz - ing, so di - vine,

And pour con - tempt on all my pride.
I sac - ri - fice them to His blood.
Or thorns com - pose so rich a crown?
And all the globe is dead to me.
De - mands my soul, my life, my all.

PRECIOUS MEMORIES

J. B. F. Wright, 1924

Performed by Emmylou Harris

Precious memories, unseen angels / Sent from somewhere to my soul
How they linger ever near me / And the sacred scenes unfold

Precious father, loving mother / Fly across the lonely years
And those old home scenes of my childhood / In fond memory appear

Precious memories, how they linger / How they ever flood my soul
In the stillness of the midnight / Precious, sacred scenes unfold

AFTER THE LOSS OF A CHILD

Although J. B. F. Wright had little or no musical education, like so many songwriters he simply drew from inspiration. Born in 1877 in Tennessee, Wright was a member of the Church of God and began writing at an early age. He penned "Precious Memories" after his son, Everett, died at the age of 3 1/2 in 1924.

Every effort to make society sensitive to the importance of the family
is a great service to humanity.

POPE JOHN PAUL II

"Take heed to yourself, and diligently keep yourself, lest you forget the things your eyes have seen, and lest they depart from your heart all the days of your life. And teach them to your children and your grandchildren."

DEUTERONOMY 4:9

I will remember the works of the LORD;
Surely I will remember Your wonders of old.
I will also meditate on all Your work,
And talk of Your deeds.

PSALM 77:11, 12

But Timothy has just now come to us from you and has brought good news about your faith and love. He has told us that you always have pleasant memories of us and that you long to see us, just as we also long to see you.

1 THESSALONIANS 3:6 NIV

HYMN NOTES

"Precious Memories" has found popularity from a diverse range of mainstream artists. Bob Dylan recorded the song for his Knocked Out Loaded *album, which released in 1986. It was also a bonus track on Bruce Springsteen's* Lost Masters Vol. I: Alone in Colts Neck, *an album completely consisting of acoustic home demos. Willie Nelson, Tennessee Ernie Ford, and The Stanley Brothers also took their turns recording the beloved song.*

TURN YOUR EYES UPON JESUS

Helen Howarth Lemmel, 1922

Through death into life everlasting / He passed, and we follow Him there;
Over us sin no more hath dominion / For more than conquerors we are!

Turn your eyes upon Jesus, / Look full in His wonderful face,
And the things of earth will grow strangely dim / In the light of His glory and grace.

'DICTATED BY THE HOLY SPIRIT'

Helen H. Lemmel (1863-1961) came to America from England at the age of 12. She was a talented singer who studied abroad in Germany. She married, but her husband left her when she became blind. She eventually got a job teaching music at the Moody Bible Institute of Chicago.

In 1918, a missionary friend had given her an evangelistic pamphlet entitled "Focused," written by Lillian Trotter. Within the Gospel tract she found these words: "So then, turn your eyes upon Him, look full into His face and you will find that the things of earth will acquire a strange new dimness." Helen couldn't stop thinking about those words. After reading the pamphlet Helen recalled, "Suddenly, as if commanded to stop and listen, I stood still, and singing in my soul and spirit was the chorus, with not one conscious moment of putting word to word to make rhyme, or note to note to make melody. The verses were written the same week, after the usual manner of composition, but none the less dictated by the Holy Spirit."

"Turn Your Eyes Upon Jesus" was only one of nearly 500 hymns Helen Lemmel wrote during her 97 years of life.

Therefore we also, since we are surrounded by so great a cloud of witnesses, let us lay aside every weight, and the sin which so easily ensnares us, and let us run with endurance the race that is set before us, looking unto Jesus, the author and finisher of our faith, who for the joy that was set before Him endured the cross, despising the shame, and has sat down at the right hand of the throne of God. For consider Him who endured such hostility from sinners against Himself, lest you become weary and discouraged in your souls.

HEBREWS 12:1—3

Let not your heart be troubled; you believe in God, believe also in Me.

In My Father' house are many mansions; if it were not so, I would have told you. I go to prepare a place for you.

And if I go and prepare a place for you, I will come again and receive you to Myself; that where I am, there you may be also.

And where I go you know, and the way you know.

JOHN 14:1-4

You will keep him in perfect peace, whose mind is stayed on You, because he trusts in You.

ISAIAH 26:3

Turn Your Eyes Upon Jesus

Helen H. Lemmel

Helen H. Lemmel

1. O soul, are you wea - ry and trou - bled? No light in the
2. Thro' death in - to life ev - er - last - ing He passed, and we
3. His word shall not fail you He prom - ised; Be - lieve Him, and

dark-ness you see? There's light for a look at the Sav - ior, And
fol - low Him there; O - ver us sin no more hath do - min - ion For
all will be well; Then go to a world that is dy - ing, His

life more a - bun - dant and free!
per - fect sal - va - tion to tell!

Turn your eyes up - on Je - sus,

Look full in His won - der - ful face,

And the things of

earth Will grow strange-ly dim In the light of His glo - ry and grace.

'I SURRENDER ALL

Judson W. Van DeVenter, 1896

All to Jesus I surrender / All to Him I freely give;
I will ever love and trust Him / In His presence daily live.

I surrender all. I surrender all.
All to Thee, my blessed Saviour,
I surrender all.

'GOD HAD HIDDEN A SONG IN MY HEART'

Born on a farm in Michigan in 1855, Judson W. Van DeVenter (1855-1939) grew up to become an enthusiastic art teacher, teaching high school in Sharon, Pennsylvania. But as his professional life grew, so did his passion for music. He sang in the choir at the local Methodist Episcopal church. For years, friends who were impressed by his musical abilities encouraged him to enter full-time music ministry, but Judson wasn't sure. He struggled to make the right decision.

Eventually, he began traveling throughout the United States, England and Scotland, ministering through music at evangelistic rallies. It was during one such meeting in East Palestine, Ohio, that Judson wrote the now famous hymn "I Surrender All."

Of the writing of the hymn, Judson wrote, "For some time, I had struggled between developing my talents in the field of art and going into full-time evangelistic work. At last the pivotal hour of my life came, and I surrendered all. A new day was ushered into my life. I became an evangelist and discovered down deep in my soul a talent hitherto unknown to me. God had hidden a song in my heart, and touching a tender chord, He caused me to sing."

But now, O LORD, You are our Father; we are the clay,
and You our potter; and we all are the work of Your
hand.

ISAIAH 64:8

"Only in the Christian life does surrender bring victory."
ANONYMOUS

HYMN NOTES

While teaching hymnology in the 1930s at Florida Bible Institute (now Trinity Bible College), J.W. Van De Venter greatly influenced an eager student named Billy Graham, who later acknowledged Van De Venter's impact on his early preaching.

"So likewise, whoever of you does not forsake all that he has cannot be My disciple."

LUKE 14:33

I Surrender All

Judson W. Van De Venter

Winfield S. Weeden

1. All to Je-sus I sur-ren-der, All to Him I free-ly give;
2. All to Je-sus I sur-ren-der, Hum-bly at His feet I bow,
3. All to Je-sus I sur-ren-der, Make me Sav-ior whol-ly Thine;
4. All to Je-sus I sur-ren-der, Lord, I give my-self to Thee.

I will ev-er love and trust Him, In His pres-ence dai-ly live.
World-ly pleas-ures all for-sak-en, Take me, Je-sus, take me now.
Let me feel the Ho-ly Spir-it, Tru-ly know that Thou art mine.
Fill me with Thy love and pow-er; Let Thy bless-ings fall on me.

I sur-ren-der all, I sur-ren-der all.
I sur-ren-der all, I sur-ren-der all.

All to Thee my bless-ed Sav-ior, I sur-ren-der all.

CONCLUSION

"Let the Amen sound from His people again . . ."

FROM "PRAISE TO THE LORD, THE ALMIGHTY"
written by Joachim Neander in 1680; translated into English by Catherine Winkworth

In today's frantic and uncertain world, rediscovering these incomparable hymns make us realize that the same God who breathed these beautiful words into the psalmists of ages past is the same God who whispers His grace over our doorways, His blessing by our bedsides and His truth in our hearts. God has not changed. His truth has not changed. How powerfully these timeless truths so incredibly displayed in this heritage of song, continue to impact generation after generation.

May "all that have life and breath come now with praises before Him, gladly for aye we adore Him."

> One generation will commend Your works to another; they will tell of Your mighty acts. They will speak of the glorious splendor of Your majesty, and I will meditate on Your wonderful works.
>
> PSALM 145:4, 5

ACKNOWLEDGMENTS

Morgan, Robert J. *Then Sings My Soul: 150 of the World's Greatest Hymn Stories.* Nashville, Thomas Nelson, 2003.

Osbeck, Kenneth W. *101 Hymn Stories.* Grand Rapids: Kregel Publications, 1982.

The following web sites were most helpful in compiling research for this project:

www.africana.com
www.Cyberhymnal.org
www.honkytonks.org
www.Hymnuts.com
www.hymnsite.com
http://justusanglican.org
www.mercer.edu/baptiststudies
www.MSN.com
www.negrospirituals.com

www.PBS.org
www.Sonymusic.com
The Southern Gospel Music Association
www.sgma.org
www.Tanbible.com
www.touchedbyelvis.com
www.wikipedia.org
www.weddingguide.co.uk
www.worshipmusic.com

The publisher wishes to thank the following artists for sharing their insights and their love of hymns in this book:

John Anderson
John Berry
Charlie Daniels
Billy Dean
Natalie Grant
Buddy Jewell
Paul Overstreet
Squire Parsons, Jr.
Marty Rayborn
Lari White

I will sing to the Lord as long as I live;
I will sing praise to my God
while I have my being.

PSALM 104:33

EXPERIENCE MORE
'AMAZING GRACE'

*with these three albums of great gospel hymns
performed by country music stars.*

Amazing Grace 1
Entire album
is included
in this book!

Amazing Grace 2   Amazing Grace 3